Photographs by Jane Burton

# Puppies

## Wet Noses and Fuzzy Bellies

*Golden Retriever (8 weeks)*

Editorial Project: Valeria Manferto De Fabianis - Graphic Design: Clara Zanotti

Preface: Giorgio Ferrero - Editorial Assistant: Giorgio Ferrero

The Publisher would like to thank Nanni Trivellone
and Luciana Perasso for their helpful collaboration

# **Puppies** Wet Noses and Fuzzy Bellies

“Many people will walk
in and out of your life,
but only true friends will leave
footprints in your heart.”

(Eleanor Roosevelt)

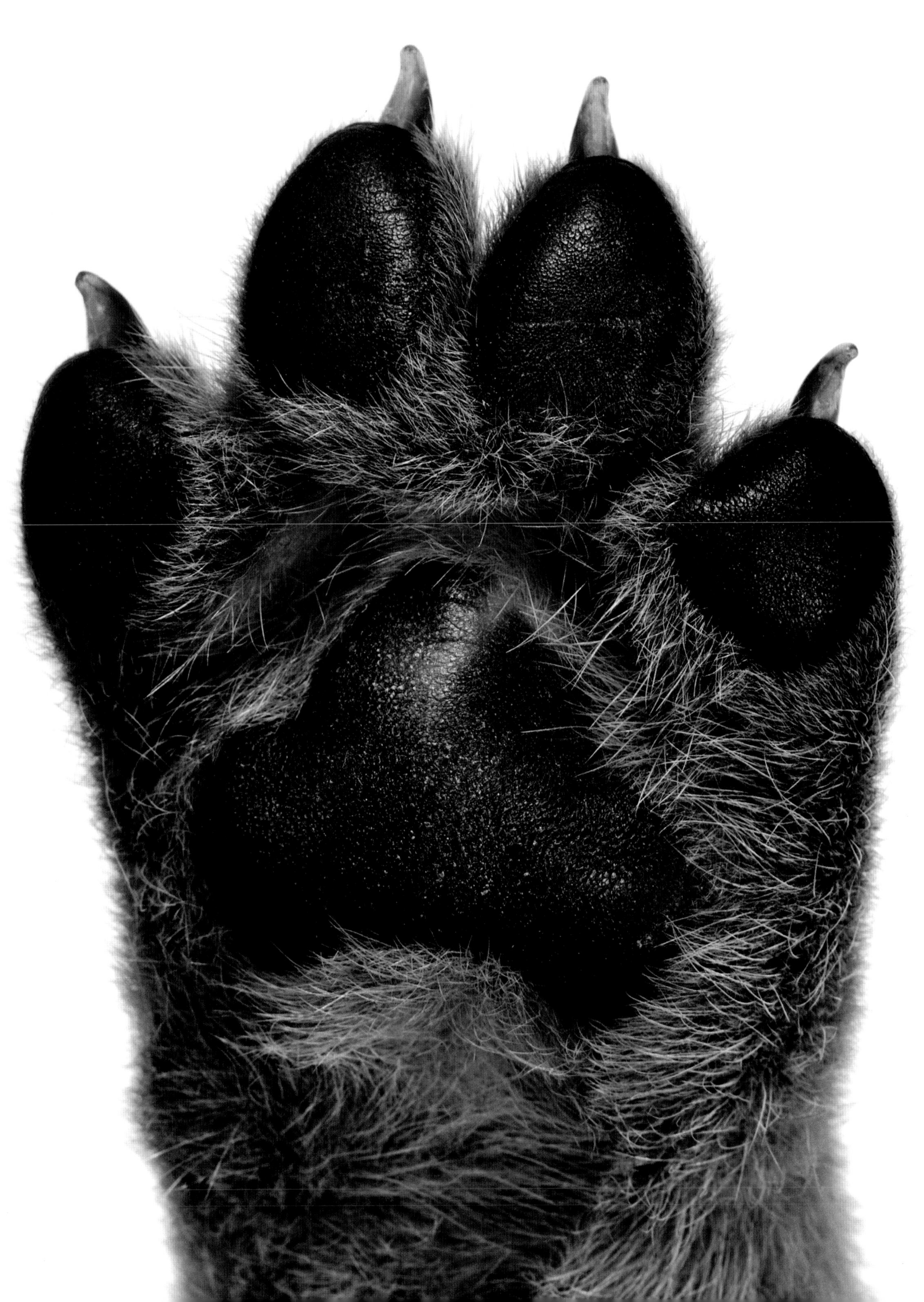

Preface by
GIORGIO FERRERO

**At first sight, they may appear to be miniature dogs, but in reality, they are puppies. Small, affectionate, sleepy, curious, playful, insatiable... and much more. Each has its own personality and they are all utterly irresistible. Puppies grow up fast and learn from their experiences and relationships with their mothers and their brothers and sisters. They soon become adults, but it is during the initial phase of their life that**

“Happiness is a warm puppy.”

(Charles M. Schulz)

As with the offspring of many species, during the first weeks of their life, puppies require the constant presence of their mother, who nourishes and attends to them and warms and comforts them. But they will soon start discovering the world, mainly through playing and through their relationships with others. And so, brothers and sisters, or a simple object found in the home, become the protagonists of important experiences and learning adventures for the puppies, but most especially they become incomparable occasions that provide entertainment to onlookers. Every expression, each movement - even the most uncoordinated one - seems designed to attract attention, conquer the observer and make him/her fall in love with the puppy. And yet it is all so natural and spontaneous. Simply disarming. The puppy observes, sniffs, explores and lies down with tummy facing upwards. Or he plays, wrestles with his brothers and sisters, rolls around and stretches his paws. He sleeps peacefully or tosses and turns while dreaming. And by doing this, the puppy always reveals a new aspect of himself, his character and his canine nature. One could watch puppies for hours, fascinated by this world filled with tumbles and sweet expressions. Indeed, one should never miss the chance to observe them because puppies grow up fast and soon become adults. Those who aren't lucky enough to have a puppy in their house can leaf through the pages of this book in the meantime...

FAST FOOD

*Dalmatian (7 weeks)*

THE BEAUTY OF BEING A PUPPY

*Dalmatian (15 days)*

“Us two in the room, my dog and me [...]
I understand that at this instant there is living in him and in me the same feeling,
that there is no difference between us.
We are the same;
in each of us there burns and shines the same trembling spark [...] No!
We are not beast and man that glance at one another [...]
They are the eyes of equals, those eyes riveted on one another.
And in each of these, in the beast and in the man,
the same life huddles up in fear close to the other.”

(Ivan Turgenev)

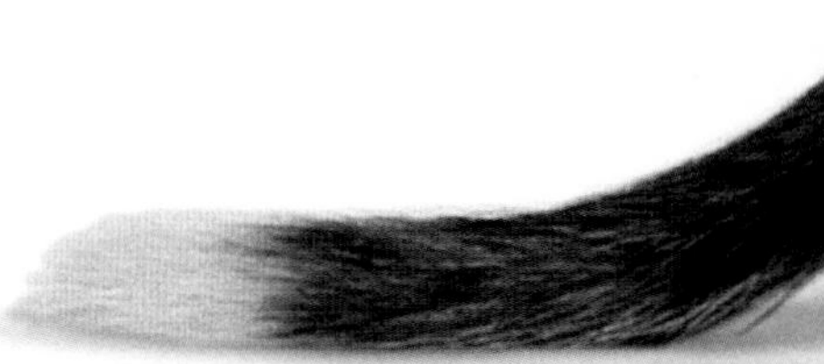

*Mixed breed (6 weeks)*

“My face is my passport.”
(Vladimir Horowitz)

*Bulldog (8 weeks)*

“I am neither an optimist nor pessimist, but a possibilist.”
(Max Lerner)

*Shar-Pei (8/9 weeks)*

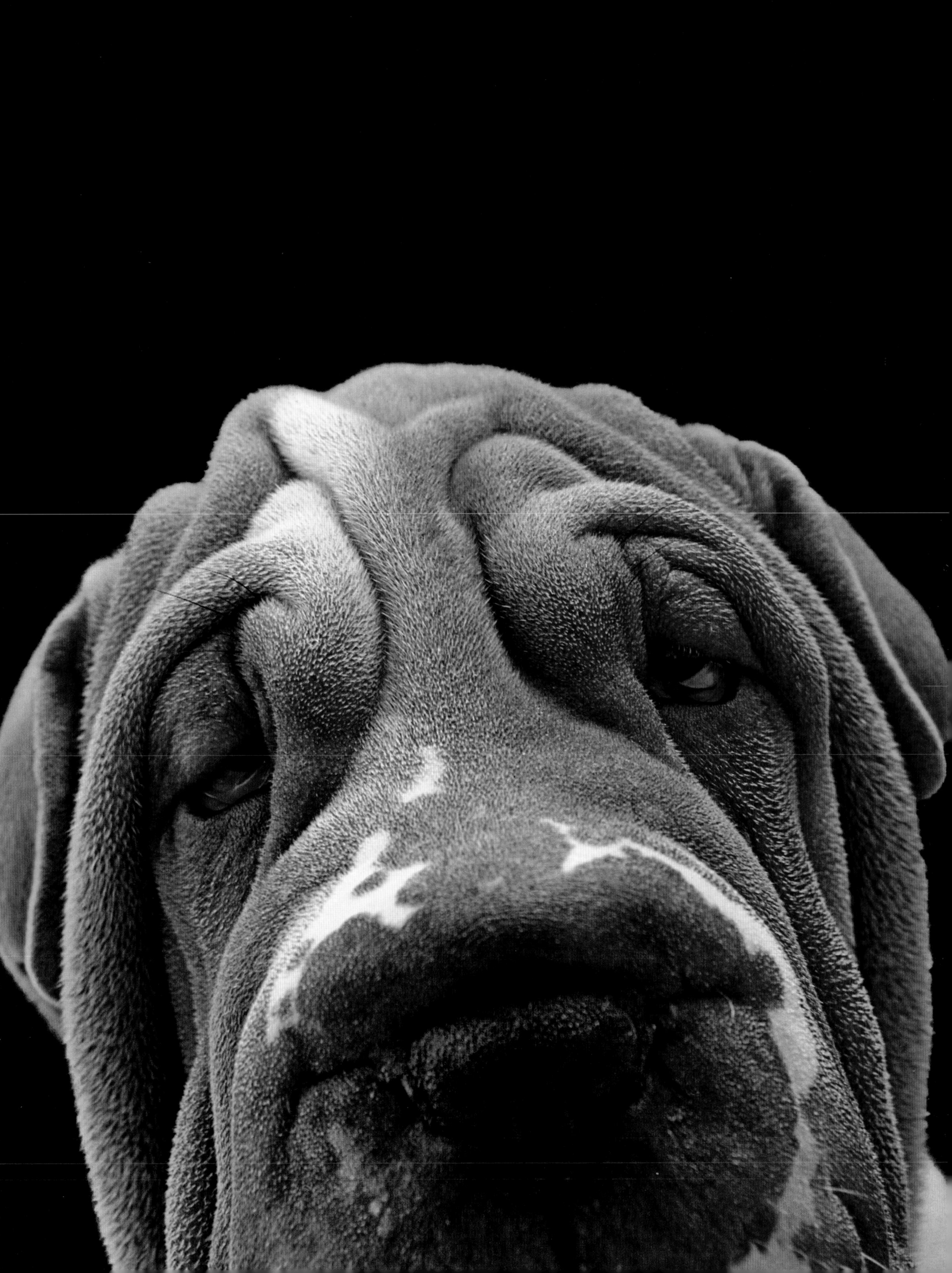

*Alaskan Malamute (7 weeks)*

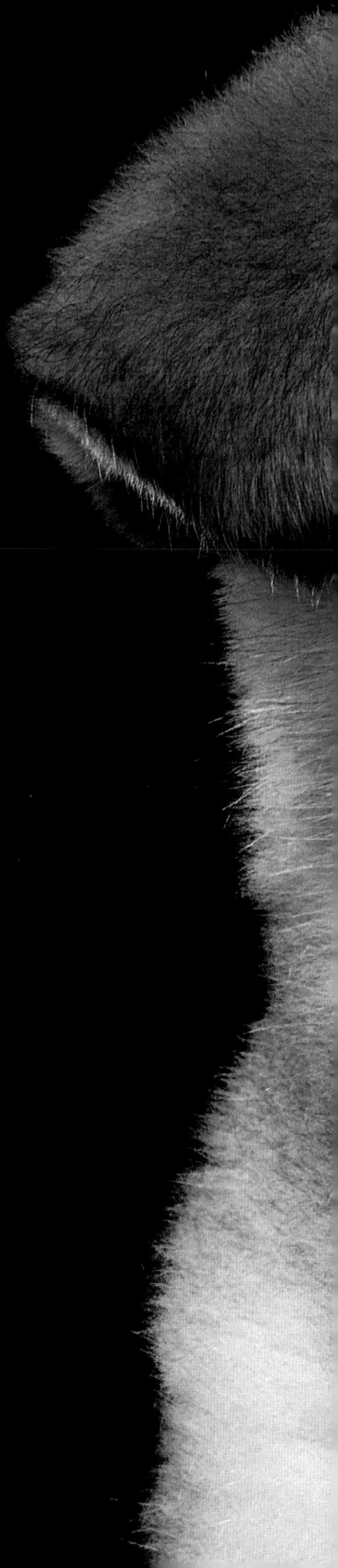

“There is no psychiatrist in the world
like a puppy licking your face.”
(Bern Williams)

# THE KING OF THE SAVANNAH

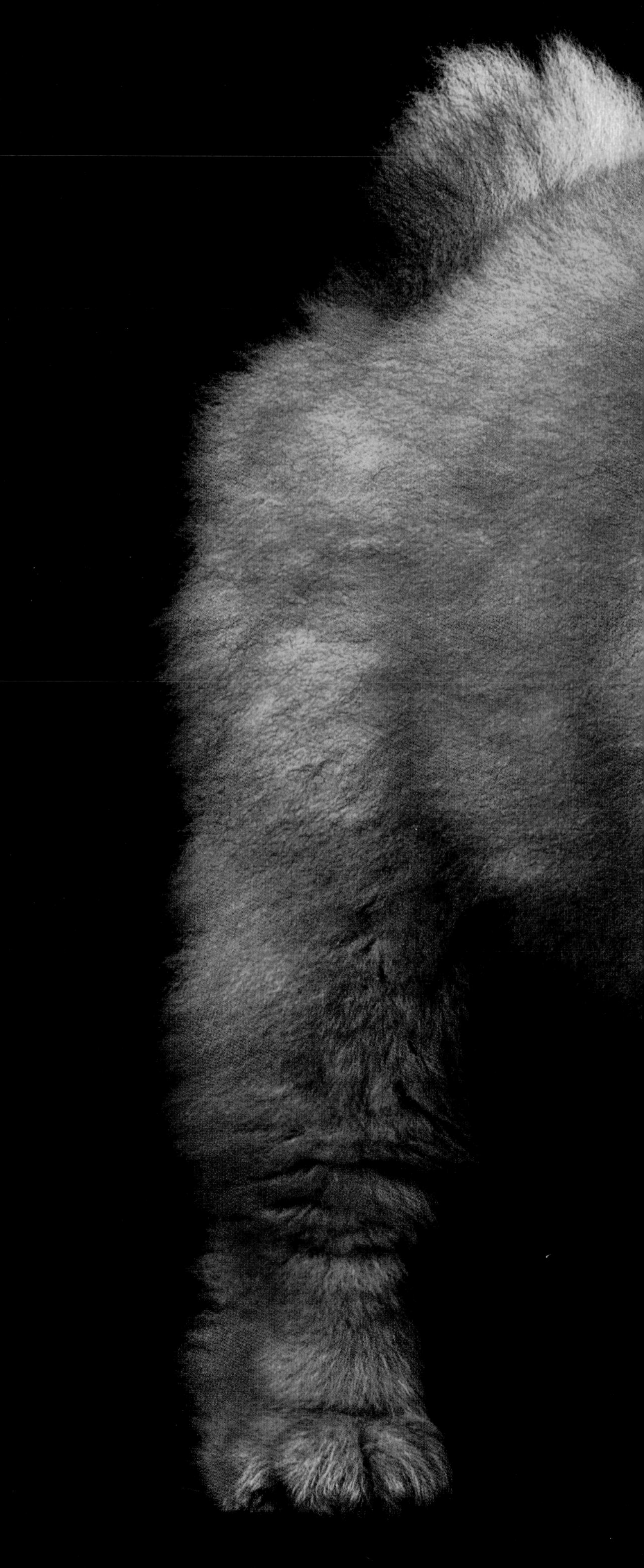

*Chow-Chow (8 weeks)*

“Every dog is a lion at home.”
(H.G. Bohn)

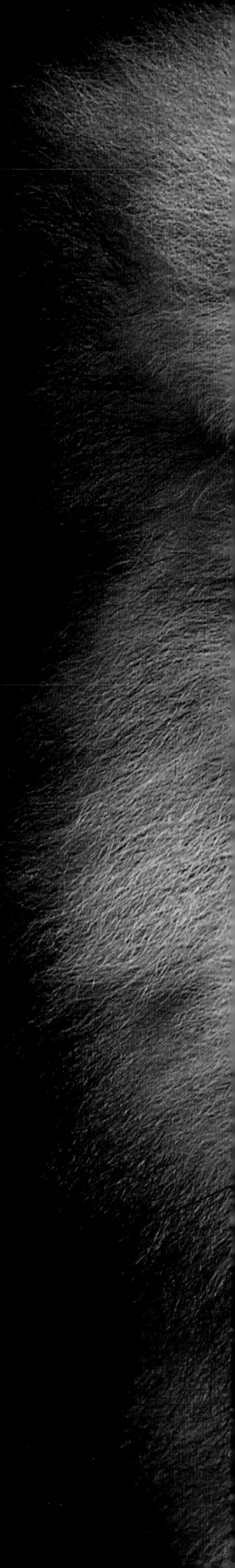

*Chow-Chow (8 weeks)*

THE BLUES BROTHERS

*Boxer (7/8 weeks)*

*Border Collie (10 weeks)*

Borzoi (10 weeks)

"A smile is...

*Hungarian Vizsla (7 weeks)*

… an inexpensive way to improve your look." (Charles Gordy)

*Boxer (5/6 weeks)*

# MELODRAMA

*Bear Coat Shar-Pei (11 weeks)*

"Each of us has heaven and hell in him."
(Oscar Wilde)

*Siberian Husky (9 weeks) - Border Collie (9 weeks)*

## THE FOUR MUSKETEERS

*Beagle (12 weeks) - English Mastiff (6 weeks)*

# FRAMES

*Bulldog (8 weeks)*

*Newfoundland (6 weeks)*

# DARK SOUL

“Without wearing any mask we are conscious of,...

*Bulldog (6 weeks)*

… we have a special face for each friend.” (Oliver Wendell Holmes)

*Border Terrier (7 weeks) and Labradoodle (8/9 weeks)*



## REBELLIOUS... CONFORMIST

“The bashful are always aggressive at heart.”

(Charles Horton Cooley)

*Bulldog (5 weeks)*

SUNROOM

*Great Dane (4 weeks)*

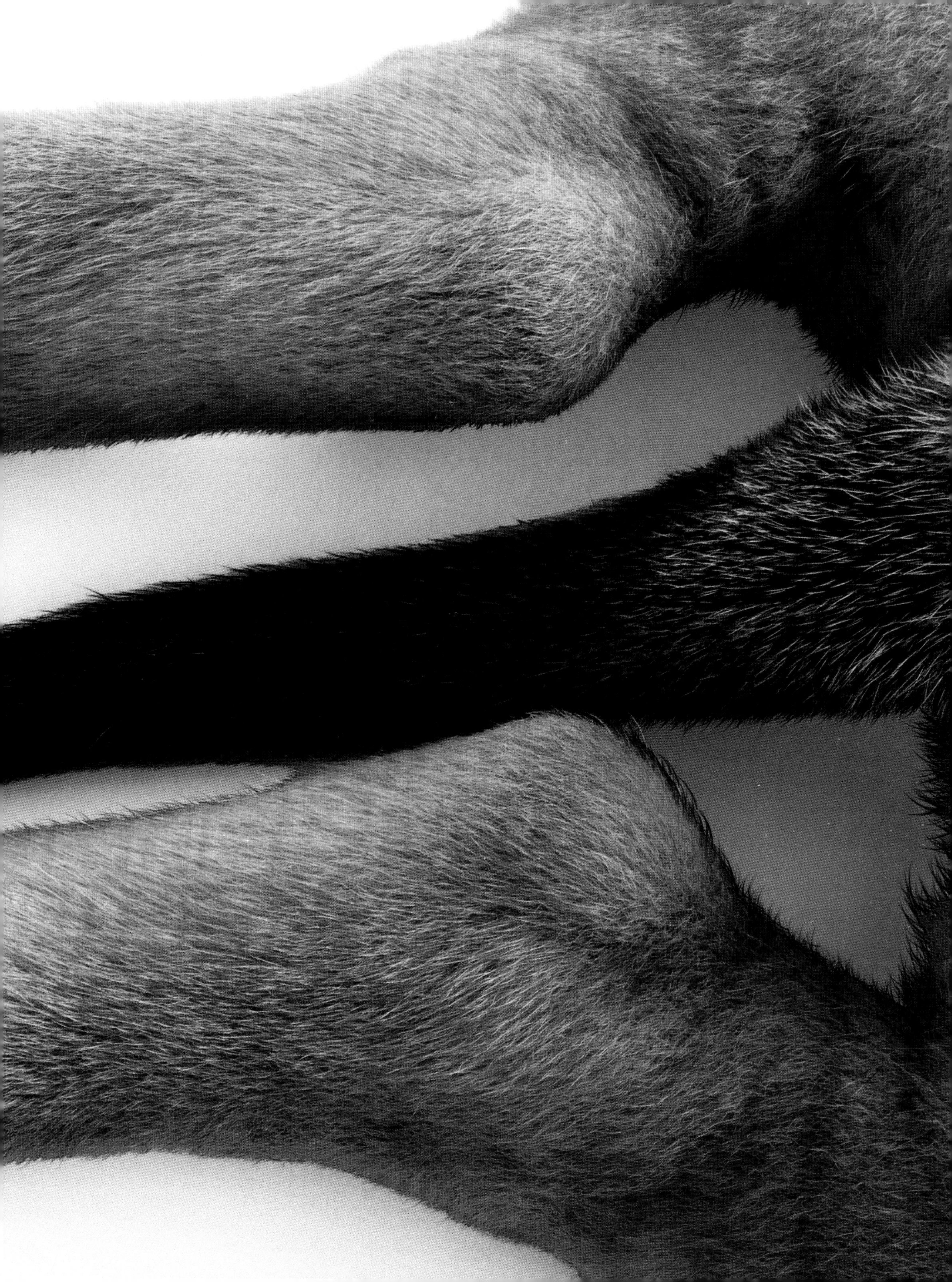

*Dachshund (9 weeks)*

“A Sabbath well spent, brings a week of content.” (English proverb)

"You can say any foolish thing to a dog, and the dog will give you this look that says,



*Chesapeake Bay Retriever (5/6 weeks)*

'My God, you're right! I never would've thought of that!'." (Dave Barry)

German Shepherd (7 weeks)

AEROBICS LESSON

"Stare into your dog's eyes and try to say that animals have no soul."

(Victor Hugo)



*Border Collie (8 weeks)*

*Hungarian Vizsla (8 weeks)*

# THE BURDEN OF RESPONSIBILITY

“Even the fall of a dancer is a somersault.” (Sri Lankan proverb)

*Shetland Sheepdog (7 weeks)*

*Bulldog (8 weeks)*

“If you obey all the rules, you miss all the fun.”

(Katharine Hepburn)

“Puppies are nature’s remedy for feeling unloved.”
(Richard Allan Palm)



*Boxer (9 weeks)*

“I always made an awkward bow.” (John Keats)

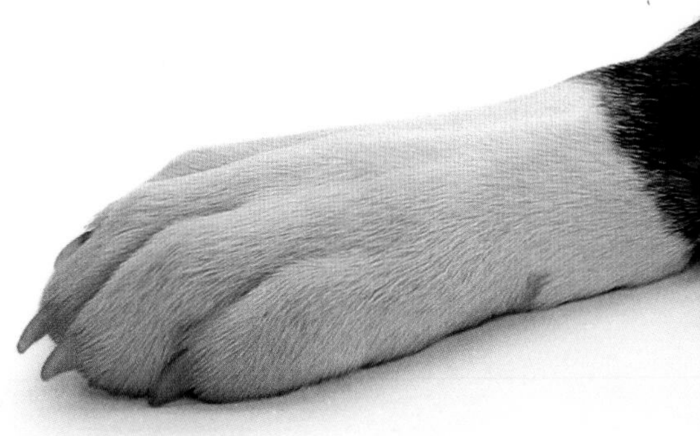

*Boxer (9 weeks)*

TIP-TAP

*Mix of Westie and Jack Russell Terrier (9 weeks)*

Mix of Labrador and Portuguese Water Dog (12/14 weeks)

“Gunfight at the O.K. Corral.” (John Sturges)

*Shar-Pei (8 weeks)*

"Cunning is a short blanket.
If you pull it over your face, you expose your feet."

(English proverb)

“I am so very proud of all my wrestlers.
They performed like warriors.”

(Patrick Kelly)



*Shar-Pei (7 weeks)*

# QUESTION TIME

*Great Dane (9 weeks)*

OLD SEA DOG

*English Mastiff (6 weeks)*

*Belgian Sheepdog (10 weeks)*

WITH A DANCING STEP

"If I were not a man, then I should wish to be a dog."

(Alexander the Great)

*German Shepherd (12 weeks)*

DESTINED FOR GREAT UNDERTAKINGS

*St. Bernard (8 weeks)*

# GUILTY FEELINGS

*Belgian Sheepdog (10 weeks)*

“A dog has the soul of a philosopher.”
(Plato)

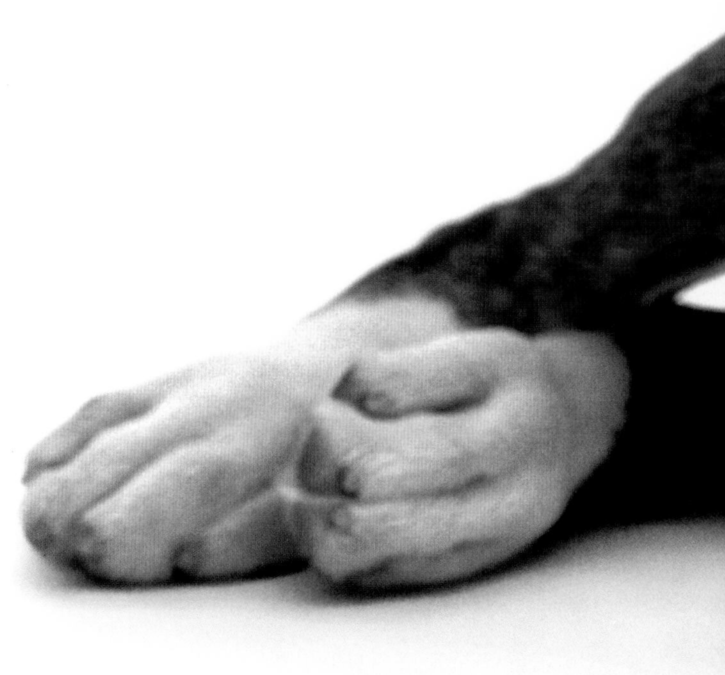

*Boxer (9 weeks)*

"If a dog's prayers were answered, bones would rain from the sky."

(English proverb)

*American Staffordshire Terrier (9/10 weeks)*

# ROMEO AND JULIET

CAN YOU GUESS WHO I AM?

*Siberian Husky (6 weeks)*

*Newfoundland (7 weeks)*

## RECIPROCAL SUPPORT

*Bulldog (8/9 weeks)*

“The most beautiful discovery true friends make is that they can grow separately without growing apart.”

(Elisabeth Foley)

*Cocker Spaniel (8 weeks) and Border Terrier (9/10 weeks)*

"Stolen kisses are always sweetest."
(Leigh Hunt)

*English Springer Spaniel (7 weeks)*

“There's none so deaf as those who will not hear.”

(Italian proverb)

*Dachshund (10 weeks)*

Pekingese (12/14 weeks) and English Mastiff (6 weeks)

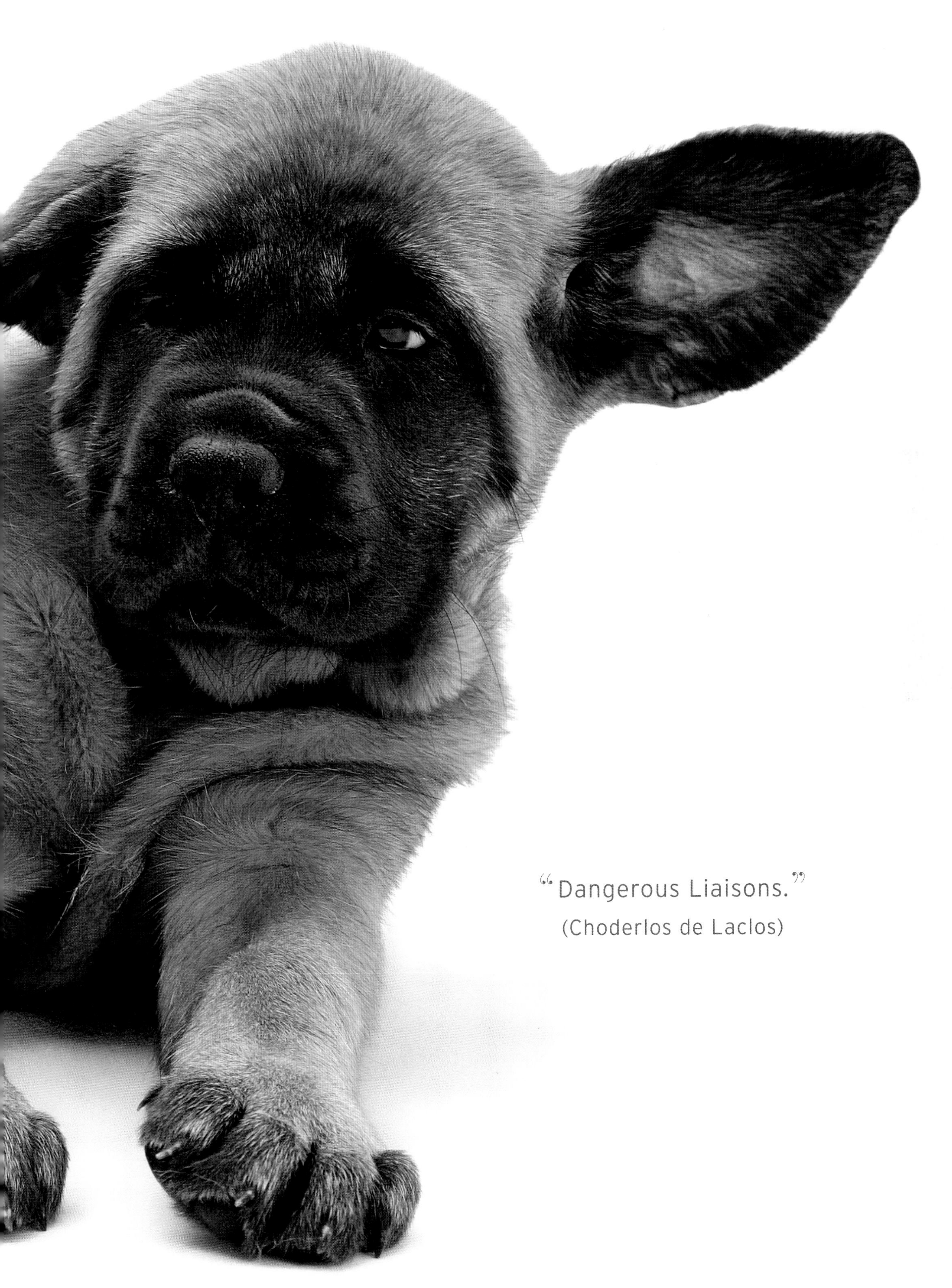

"Dangerous Liaisons."
(Choderlos de Laclos)

*Dalmatian (7 weeks)*

# POWER GAMES

*Labrador (7/8 weeks)*

AN EYE FOR AN EYE...

*Staffordshire Bull Terrier (6 weeks)*

*Golden Retriever (5/6 weeks)*

"For the friendship of two, the patience of one is required."

(Indian proverb)

*Newfoundland (6 weeks)*

“Surrender is rarely good strategy.”
(Ben Manski)

*Dalmatian (5 weeks)*

## GRECO-ROMAN WRESTLING

*Shar-Pei (5/7 weeks)*

"If you learn from defeat, you haven't really lost."
(Zig Ziglar)

*Cocker Spaniel (8 weeks)*

Epagneul Breton (6 weeks)

“If you don’t see yourself as a winner,
then you cannot perform as a winner.”

(Zig Ziglar)

“ A long dispute...

*Labrador (6 weeks)*

... means both parties are wrong.” (Voltaire)

“Nothing makes us so lonely as our secrets.” (Paul Tournier)

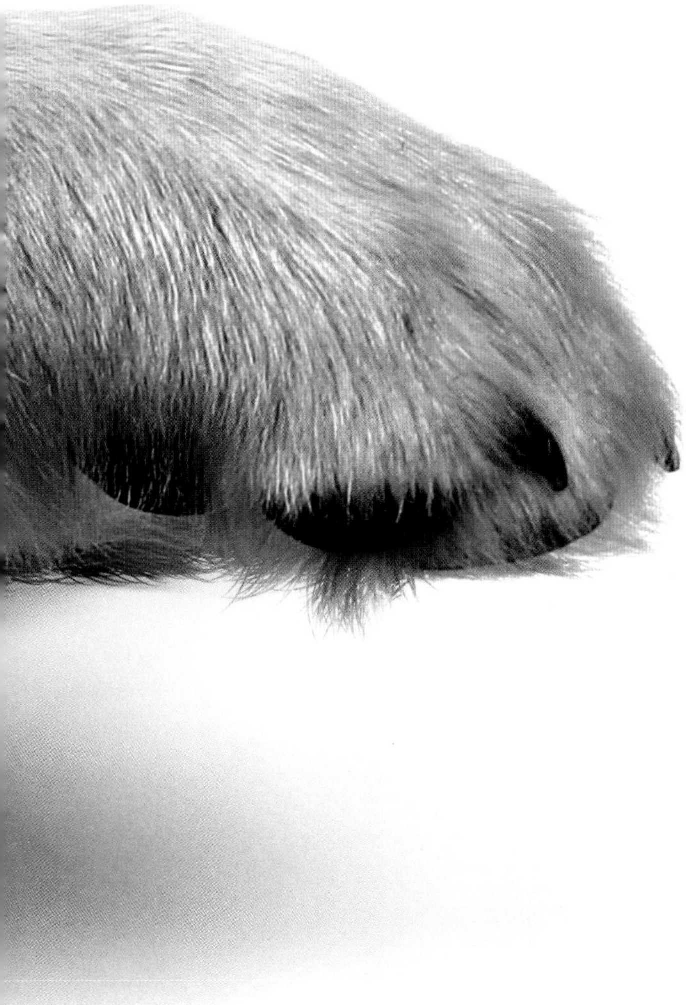

*Golden Retriever (6/7 weeks)*

"Happiness is having a scratch for every itch."

(Ogden Nash)

*Basset Hound (7 weeks)*

*Shar-Pei (7/8 weeks)*

*Shar-Pei (7/8 weeks)*

“It always seems as though a puppy...

... has more skin than truly needed.” (Maya V. Patel)

"The biggest dog has been a pup."
(Joaquin Miller)

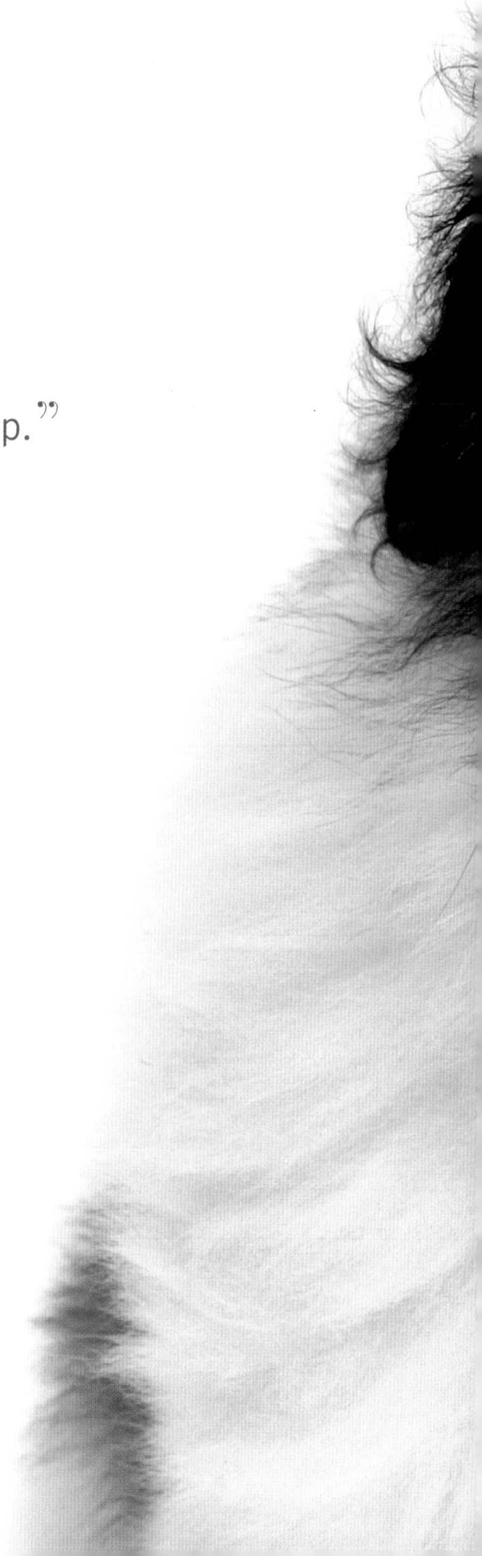

*St. Bernard (12/13 weeks)*

"If you want to sit in the most comfortable spot, have the dog get up."

(Anonymous)

"Thou shouldst eat to live, not live to eat."

(Cicero)



*Boerboel (3 weeks)*

MORNING...

*Mix of Lakeland Terrier and Border Collie (3 weeks) and Golden Retriever (4 weeks)*

... EVENING

"Please don't wake me,
no don't shake me,
leave me where I am,
I'm only sleeping."

(The Beatles - I'm Only Sleeping)

*Border Collie (14 weeks)*

"Whoever said you can't buy happiness forgot little puppies."

(Gene Hill)



*Labrador (4/5 weeks)*

"Youth comes but once in a lifetime."

(Henry Wadsworth Longfellow)

BROTHERLY HUG

*Bull Terrier (5/6 weeks)*

*Shar-Pei (7 weeks)*

*Spinone (8/9 weeks)*

"The higher we soar, the smaller we appear to those who cannot fly." (Friedrich Nietzsche)

*Basset Hound (7 weeks)*

"A long voyage begins with just one step."
(Filipino proverb)

*German Shepherd (8 weeks)*

“All truly great thoughts are conceived while walking.”
(Friedrich Nietzsche)

*Basset Hound (9 weeks)*

“I love to travel, but hate to arrive.”
(Albert Einstein)

*Bulldog (13 weeks)*

"Moving fast is not the same as going somewhere."
(Robert Anthony)



*Cocker Spaniel (12 weeks)*

"We never know the love of our parents for us till we have become parents."
(Henry Ward Beecher)

*English Setter (8 weeks)*

*German Shepherd (12/13 weeks)*

# A DAY WITH THE FAMILY

CHEESE...

*German Shepherd (9/10 weeks and 20/21 weeks)*

"Children have more need of models than of critics."
(Carolyn Coats)

*Golden Retriever (7 weeks) and Saluki (9/10 weeks)*

“A dog is like an eternal Peter Pan,
a child who never grows...”
(Aaron Katcher)

"The family is one of nature's masterpieces."

(George Santayana)

*Labrador (4/5 weeks)*

Lurcher (3 weeks)

CUDDLES BY TURNS

“Children learn to smile from their parents.”

(Shinichi Suzuki)

*Siberian Husky (6 weeks)*

*Dalmatian (3/4 weeks)*

101 DALMATIANS

"There's so much room for growth..."
(Chad Anderson)

*Dalmatian (3/4 weeks)*

"A mother's arms are made of tenderness,
and children sleep soundly in them."
(Victor Hugo)

*Great Dane (3 weeks)*

“The art of teaching is the art of assisting discovery.” (Mark Van Doren)

*Siberian Husky (4/5 weeks)*

*Utonagan (6/7 weeks)*

## NEW GENERATIONS

"Children are the anchors that hold a mother to life."

(Sophocles)

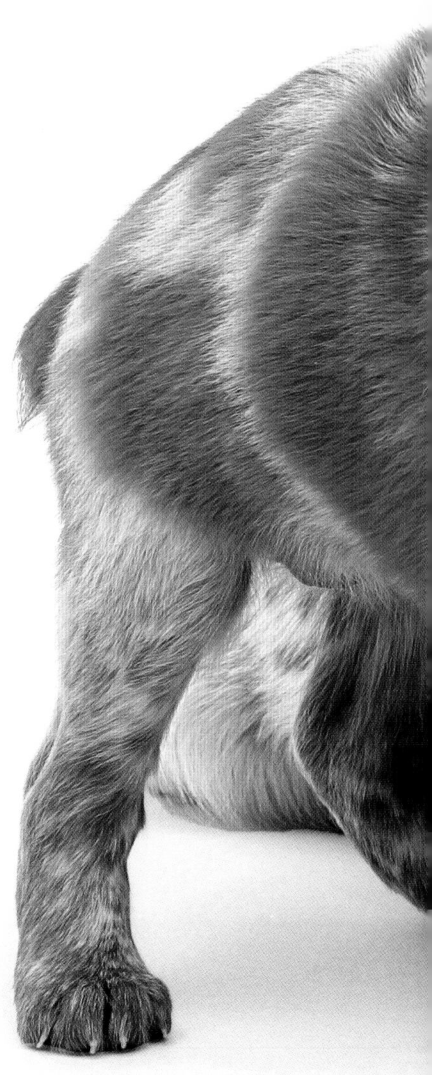

*Epagneul Breton (6/7 weeks)*

Labrador (6/7 weeks)

“You have to dream before your dreams can come true.”

(Abdul Kalam)

"If you follow every dream you might get lost."

(Neil Young - The Painter)

*German Shepherd (8 weeks)*

"Let sleeping dogs lie." (Italian proverb)

*Bulldog (4/5 weeks)*

THE SMALL HOURS

*Rottweiler (4 weeks)*

“A dream you dream alone is only a dream...

*Utonagan (6/7 weeks)*

... a dream you dream together is real." (Yoko Ono - Now or Never)

*Golden Retriever (4 weeks)*

"Tell me whom you sleep with and
I shall tell you whom you dream of."
(Stanislaw J. Lec)

"If you call a tail a leg, how many legs has a dog? Four!

*Golden Retriever (6/7 weeks)*

Calling a tail a leg doesn't make it a leg.” (Abraham Lincoln)

Labrador (5/6 weeks)

*Border Collie (5 weeks)*

ROUND TRIP

"These dogs don't require a lot of space...

*Labrador (5 weeks)*

… they curl up and go to sleep.” (Joan Ray)

"You lead a dog's life people say - but why?
You do whatever you want;
you sleep before every meal, and after..."

(A. P. Herbert)

*Labrador (5 weeks)*

"Dogs are wiser than men. They do not set great store upon things. They do not waste their days hoarding property. They do not ruin their sleep worrying about how to keep the objects they have, and to obtain the objects they have not."

(Eugene O'Neill)



*Border Collie (5 weeks)*

*Border Collie (5 weeks)*

Epagneul Breton (6/7 weeks)

WEEKEND

*Golden Retriever (5 weeks)*

“The great silence of dogs consoles us from the futile words of man.”
(Jean-Michel Chaumont)

VMB Publishers® is a registered trademark
property of Edizioni White Star s.r.l.


Via Candido Sassone, 24
13100 Vercelli, Italy
www.whitestar.it

Translation: Donna St. John
Editing: Emma Greenwood



ISBN: 978-88-540-1511-1
1 2 3 4 5 6   14 13 12 11 10

Printed in China

## PHOTO CREDITS

Joey Berg/Getty Images: pages 90-91 * Jane Burton/Warren Photographic: pages 1, 8, 11, 13, 26-27, 28, 29, 33, 36 left, 36 right, 37 right, 38-39, 42, 43, 52-53, 56-57, 65, 66-67, 68, 69, 76-77, 78-79, 82-83, 88-89, 92-93, 94-95, 98-99, 102-103, 106-107, 108-109, 110-111, 112, 112-113, 114-115, 118-119, 120-121, 122-123, 124-125, 126-127, 130-131, 132, 133, 138-139, 142, 143, 152, 153, 154-155, 160-161, 170-171, 172-173, 174-175, 176-177, 178-179, 180-181, 182-183, 187, 188-189, 190-191, 194-195, 198-199, 200-201, 202-203, 204-205, 208-209, 212-213, 214-215, 216-217, 218-219, 223 * Jim Craigmyle/Corbis: pages 46-47, 196-197 * John Daniels/KimballStock: pages 58-59 * Datacraft/Getty Images: pages 150-151 * Araldo De Luca/Archivio White Star: pages 3, 16, 20-21, 22-23, 24-25, 40, 41, 96-97, 116-117, 148-149, 156-157, 164-165, 166-167, 168-169, 192-193, 206-207, 220-221, 224 * Pat Doyle/Corbis: pages 30, 31 * Patricia Doyle/Getty Images: page 15 * Fancy/Veer/Corbis: pages 45, 147 * Fotototo/Blickwinkel: pages 50-51, 72-73, 75, 128-129 * Yasuhide Fumoto/Getty Images: page 19 * Martin Harvey/Getty Image: pages 7, 48-49, 141, 184-185 * Ron Kimball/KimballStock: pages 32, 104-105, 134-135 * J. M. Labat/ardea.com: pages 62-63 * Sharon Montrose/Getty Images: pages 4, 5 * Neo Vision/Getty Images: pages 210-211 * Martin Rogers/KimballStock: pages 34, 35 * Mark Taylor/Warren Photographic: pages 37 left, 44, 54-55, 60-61, 70, 71, 80-81, 84-85, 86-87, 100, 136-137, 145, 158-159, 162, 163